SIMPLE
EXPLANATION

of

WORK IDEAS

SIMPLE EXPLANATION

of

WORK IDEAS

by
Maurice Nicoll

*from Beryl Pogson's papers
based on the Teachings of
G.I. Gurdjieff
P.D. Ouspensky
& Maurice Nicoll*

Published in Great Britain by
ASHGROVE PRESS LIMITED
Bath Road, Norton St Philip
Bath BA3 6 LW

This edition 1996
Reprinted 1998

ISBN NUMBER 1–85398–081–1

The sale of this book will benefit the
MACMILLAN NURSES
Cancer Relief Macmillan Fund
Anchor House 15 Britten Street
LONDON SW3 3TZ

Printed in Great Britain by Redwood Books
Trowbridge, Wiltshire

Beryl Pogson and Maurice Nicoll, 1949

"The Teaching is to prepare people for the Aquarian Age where all religions can be united - united by the fundamental truths contained in every religion."

Beryl Pogson (More Work Talks 1966, p93)

SIMPLE EXPLANATION
of
WORK IDEAS
Maurice Nicoll
1884-1953

BERYL POGSON had this *Simple Explanation of Work Ideas* by Dr Maurice Nicoll amongst her papers. In the 1950s she read them to her groups and discussions followed. I remember her telling me that she arrived at The Knapp, Birdlip in Gloucestershire on 28 May 1940 with Dr and Mrs Nicoll, having left Tyeponds in Essex as Colonel Butler had warned them that Lakes Farm and Tyeponds were to be taken over by the Military, and that this was shortly to become a military zone; it was expected that it would be on an invasion route. The move to the Cotswolds was accomplished with great speed.

I was told that the *Simple Explanation of Work Ideas* was written by Maurice Nicoll soon after the Group arrived at The Knapp, at the request of Mrs Humphrey Butler because her two faithful servants, Barrow and his wife, Edith, had asked what *The Work* was about. For a more detailed account see Beryl Pogson's biography *Maurice Nicoll : A Portrait* (Chapter 8), originally published by Vincent Stuart in 1961 and republished in 1987 by Fourth Way Books, New York.

Beryl Pogson was a pupil of Dr Maurice Nicoll for nineteen years and his secretary for fourteen, during which period she was one of a small group who lived with him and Mrs Nicoll at the houses where 'The Work' was carried on: Tyeponds, Birdlip, Quaremead and Great Amwell House.

Before his death in 1953 Dr Nicoll authorized Beryl Pogson to teach 'The Work'.

> "Dr Nicoll gave his blessing to this new venture which expanded..."

By 1955 she had groups in Sussex, London, Scotland and Denmark, besides keeping in touch with isolated members; she was a tireless correspondent throughout her life.

After Dr and Mrs Nicoll's death, when Great Amwell House was sold, Beryl Pogson moved to 48 Belsize Avenue, London on 7 October 1954 and eventually to the top flat at 1a Nutley Terrace in Hampstead. There she held meetings until 16 April 1961 when she moved to an Edwardian country house and 16 acres of grounds at Upper Dicker in Sussex, known as The Dicker, which was now the residential Centre for her main Group. This expansion made possible larger opportunities for all of us. Apart from longer sessions during the festivals, the Group met mainly at weekends where accommodation was provided for sixty or more people. Large projects were completed with incredible speed. Acting, singing, making mosaics, pottery, tile decorating, mural painting, glass engraving, carpentry, weaving, archery and leather work were some of the creative activies. The house, grounds, and kitchen garden were maintained by the Group. The 'Movements' were taught. There were eight full-time residents at The Dicker.

This Centre closed in December 1976 when the leaders, Rear-Admiral and Mrs Ronald Oldham, moved with a small group to Cornwall, where intensive Teaching was given.

In 1978 St Bede's School, a charitable educational trust which now has 360 pupils, became the owners of The Dicker.

Practical work Teaching was always given. Beryl Pogson had a sense of urgency about 'The Work' and an inner certainty of what she should do. She always sought to form a Group into a focus of reality which could be used by a higher power. We saw our task, *firstly* in the continuing need to work on ourselves individually, *secondly* through sharing with the Group at meetings and in our gatherings and activities - to make *life our teacher* and *thirdly* to relate our efforts to the work of Conscious Humanity.

One example of the practical Teaching: We were given the following quotation:-

> "When we watch a child trying to walk we see its countless failures; its successes are but few. If we had to limit our observation within a narrow space of time, the sight would be cruel. But we find that in spite of its repeated failures there is an impetus of joy in the child which sustains it, in its seemingly impossible task. We see it does not think of its falls so much as its power to keep its balance, though only for a moment."
>
> *Sir Rabindranath Tagore (1861-1941)*

A talk followed explaining how we could learn to acquire a greater degree of flexibility and adaptablity in *'doing the next thing'*.

We re-read the above quotation and then were asked to give a certain period of time to relating this to ourselves. USE it. Relate it to the past, to the future, to NOW. (Beryl Pogson: "When I suggest doing something every day for a time it means to begin with; it doesn't mean for 365 days!")

During the last ten years of her life she was taking as many as six Group meetings a week, and daily meetings during sessions at The Dicker. These were quite informal lectures followed by questions, but quite often she would ask for a question at the beginning and a discussion would take its course from the question asked. At the meetings there were members of her groups who were from different backgrounds and different stages of 'The Work' yet with a unity of purpose. Her Work teaching was based on *The Psychological Commentaries on The Teaching of G.I. Gurdjieff and P.D. Ouspensky by Maurice Nicoll* and, of course, G.I. Gurdjieff's and P.D. Ouspensky's own writings; she often made connections between 'The Work' and sacred books, literature, plays and poetry as will be seen in this book.

Beryl Pogson taught that the aim of all religion is to change man's level of Being and to teach him to live according to his own divinely ordained nature. Every religion has an inner teaching which is basically the same, through which man can seek to reach his highest destiny. This Teaching is periodically renewed throughout the ages. Efforts are made to awaken man through the coming of great Teachers, by the lives of holy men and women, and the work of artists, writers, and musicians - many of whom came under the influence of esoteric schools in all lands and at all periods up to the present day.

In Beryl Pogson's book *Maurice Nicoll: A Portrait* some of her own significant experiences and events are recorded but she has not written about the private teaching Maurice Nicoll gave her which included interpretations of her dreams and his sharing with her of some of his own inner life. This tradition she continued with those who worked closely with her, which I do not propose to write more about, except to record that it was she who *'held the level'*, as she herself expressed it, thereby enabling others to see truths for themselves and to have experience of states of consciousness which in the ordinary course of their lives they might never have glimpsed. Beryl had an intuitive awareness of the psychological states of the people around her. I would like to acknowledge how much I owe her for this and for all that I received from her at Dorton House, her London flat, at The Dicker and on the many holidays with her in Europe. She had a compassionate understanding and did not forget what it was like to be young.

Under Beryl Pogson's leadership and inspired Teaching many people over the years realized the truth which she often repeated from Dr Nicoll's writing:

> "The Work is not a building, a place, a book, a system, dogma or tradition. The Work is something that lives in the hearts of men and women - if they can find it."

I am glad that Beryl Pogson's Teachings are now more widely known as many of them have been republished. We were reminded that we were being taught orally and that much is said in the oral teaching that is not found in books;

however, she was prompted on many occasions to distil her ideas and formulations into print.

I hope these *Simple Explanations of Work Ideas* by Dr Maurice Nicoll will be helpful to others who may be wondering what *"The Work"* is about.

LEWIS CREED

Maurice Nicoll with Pushti his dog in the 1930s
at Alley Cottage, Sidlesham, near Chichester

*(See Maurice Nicoll : A Portrait by Beryl Pogson
p.93 'Relationship with Ouspensky)*

HEAVEN

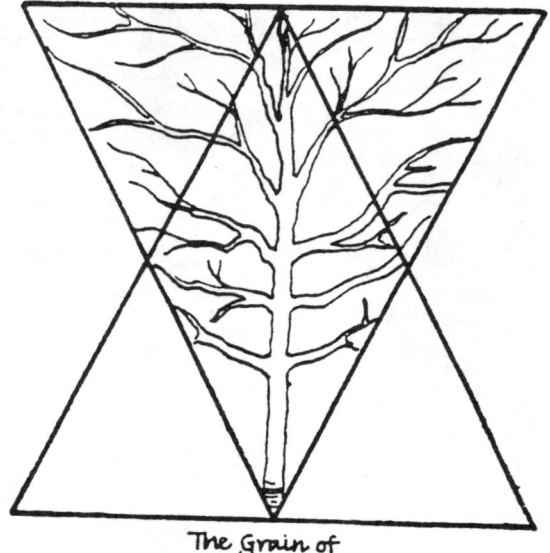

The Grain of
Mustard Seed

EARTH

The Mark p.86 by Maurice Nicoll

Beryl Pogson in the 1950s

Born 4 June 1895 at Didsbury, Lancashire
Died 5 February 1967 at The Dicker, Sussex

UNPUBLISHED PREFACE TO
THE PSYCHOLOGICAL COMMENTARIES
on the Teaching of G I Gurdjieff and P D Ouspensky
by Maurice Nicoll

This was written by Mr Fulford Bush in 1949, just before his death, at the time of the private publication of Volume I of the 'Commentaries'.

If you have undertaken what you recognize is beyond your power satisfactorily to accomplish, I can be sure of your generous reception of this attempt to convey some idea of what manner of man it is who has written this book, this series of lectures on the questions that arise in each one of us - to which we have found no answer - to which many of us have thought there is no answer - but to which the answer can be found if a man will study this book and apply to himself its Teaching.

That is a big thing to say, but it is as true as it is big, and while I acknowledge my inadequacy to give you a fitting pen picture of the author I can say without the least hesitation or reservation that when you have read this book you will realize that I have made no overstatement as to his depth of knowledge, breadth of understanding and height of purpose.

Dr Maurice Nicoll was born at Kelso, Scotland, on the 19th July 1884, the only son of Sir William Robertson Nicoll, the editor of The British Weekly, The Bookman, and the author of many books.

Maurice Nicoll was at school at Aldenham, Herts., and went to Caius College, Cambridge, from there to Barts where he qualified as a physician. He spent some years studying in Paris, Berlin and Vienna. During this time he wrote several novels and short stories. After this he began to practise in Harley Street, becoming interested in the psychological teaching of Dr Carl Jung of Zürich.

In the 1914 war he was in Gallipoli and Mesopotamia where he served with the R.A.M.C.

Being invalided back to England he was one of the medical officers in charge of the Empire Hospital in Vincent Square, a hospital for men wounded in the head and spine.

At this time he wrote many psychological papers for the B.M.A. and also had a play produced, Lord Richard in the Pantry, which ran for three years. Dr Nicoll was considering Dr Jung's request to be his representative in England when in October 1921 he met Mr P D Ouspensky in London and heard Ouspensky expound a Teaching which interested him deeply and answered for him many questions never before answered.

Later, giving up his Harley Street practice, Dr Nicoll went to an Institute at Fontainebleau run by Gurdjieff, who was Ouspensky's teacher.

Returning to England after a year at Fontainebleau he began in 1931 with Ouspensky's permission to pass on the Ideas which he had received from both Teachers. This he continues to do from Great Amwell House, near Ware, Herts., where he now lives.

I first met Dr Nicoll in the beginning of 1926 on my return from China where I had been practising law in Peking and Tientsin. He had after leaving Fontainebleau resumed his practice in Harley Street as the leading neurologist in London and my call was made upon him in his professional capacity having been advised to consult him by Mr Kenneth Walker, F.R.C.S., to whom I had put up a question of a psychological rather than a physiological nature.

"Maurice Nicoll is your man" said Walker with his characteristic directness - and so it proved.

My first impression in that to me momentous call was of a man's presence, that indefinable quality one so rarely encounters and which is unmistakable. I do not think I am easily impressed. I have met many remarkable men - in China, Japan, Germany and England, particularly in China where I saw something of the China/Japan War, the Boxer Trouble, the Russo-Japanese War. Admirals, Generals, Statesmen, War Lords, Russian, Chinese and Japanese Officials, newspaper correspondents, Chinese bandit-chiefs, Governors of Provinces, French priests and British missionaries, Intelligence Department representatives and spies of different nationalities - forceful, resourceful men who had to depend upon their individual qualities to bring them through difficult and dangerous circumstances - and of all that number I recall four men who also gave me that impression of presence:

Dr Morrison - Times Correspondent, Peking, afterwards Adviser to the Chinese Government.

Dr Jinarajadasa - Theosophist.

Lord Glenesk - when he was proprietor of the Morning Post.

A Chinese healer, who seldom left his up-country South Manchurian village, but who would have been persona grata in any company.

They all had presence, a certain inner poise, a dignity born of self-command achieved by recognition of a purposed way to some definite objective, the power of detachment enabling them to view your problem objectively. But the man I met in Harley Street had and has this quality in a more remarkable degree, I think I should say here on a higher level. Of middle height, a classically shaped head, clear cut features, light blue eyes that see right through you with understanding kindliness making any attempt at evasion or deception futile, hands capable and artistic, a voice of which the diapason holds infinite range of expression - that is an attempt to give some idea of the man - Maurice Nicoll - of whom the passing 22 years have served to intensify the impressions formed at that first interview, in the course of which I put forward the difficulty that had obsessed me for some months.

The answer was simple and direct. It involved the application of psychological force of which I - in common with the average man - thought I was already possessed. At that time there were few limits to my imagined capabilities; like most men I imagined I could do what I made up my mind to do - without any conception of what making up one's mind entails.

It was my introduction to this system of Teaching. I shall not attempt to say here what this Teaching is about - how can a vessel with the capacity of a pint contain a quart - but I - man in the average - have asked myself many questions to which I could find no answer, to which an answer was an absolute necessity for life to have any meaning. All these questions and many more arising from an expanding understanding have been answered to the measure of my understanding while the way has been indicated so to increase that measure as to enable me to digest and assimilate the answers that are there, given the desire to read what is written.

What from the very first talk I had with Dr Nicoll impressed itself upon me most strongly was and is that in this Teaching, System, or The Work - as we who study it know it - there are no dogmas to be taken on faith. The Work states certain truths, but whether they are truths for you is a matter for you to decide upon if you will think. The Work is to make you think - it does not want your unintelligent affirmation - it does not ask for that - on the contrary it demands that you do not affirm it unless and until by your own thinking you arrive at the point where for you what it says is true:- for you, howsoever others may receive it, declare it, affirm it, for you it can be true only if by thinking over it and applying it you make it intelligently your own.

H. Fulford Bush
(died 24.6.49)

See letter to Mr Bush 26.3.41. from Maurice Nicoll at Birdlip, Glos. Page 1. Psychological Commentaries on the Teaching of G I Gurdjieff and P D Ouspensky by Maurice Nicoll.

* * *

Mr Bush lived to see Volume I printed and bound, but died a few days later. The sense of urgency which had prompted him to ensure that the publication of the *Commentaries* went forward with all possible speed was a true intuition. It was the last service that he rendered to Maurice Nicoll whom he so greatly venerated as a Teacher and whose right hand he had been for eighteen years.

Beryl Pogson

On Dr Maurice Nicoll's Memorial

in Lumsden Church Scotland:

TO THE GLORY OF GOD
AND IN LOVING AND ETERNAL MEMORY OF

MAURICE NICOLL

M.B., B.C., B.A., M.R.C.S., L.R.C.P.

Born 19 July 1884
Died 30 August 1953

and of his beloved wife

CATHERINE

Born 6 November 1881
Died 13 December 1953

"He that overcometh shall inherit all things"

MAURICE NICOLL
(1884–1953)

towards the end of his life
Photograph taken by Cyril Parfit
one of his Group

Symbol of Sleeping Man from the LIBER MUTUS

SIMPLE
EXPLANATION

of

WORK IDEAS

ONE

Everyone is two people - the person we suppose ourselves to be, and what we really are. Only Self-Observation shows us this. We cannot understand that we are two people unless we begin to understand what it means to observe ourselves.

We see a world outside: that is what our senses give us. But the senses are turned outwards from oneself and cannot see what one is.

But we have an organ inside ourselves which can observe this thing called oneself. By means of it we can see our thoughts, feelings, moods. This is the beginning of becoming another person.

Our life depends on this thing called 'oneself'. If we wish to have a different life, we first of all have to realise what kind of life we have now. All forms of suffering are due to this 'oneself'. As long as we remain this 'oneself' our life cannot alter. It will always attract the same misfortunes, disappointments, and so on.

So the Work begins with seeing what one is like, what kind of person one is. For example, if we treat people without consideration for their feelings and do not know it, we shall always be suffering from their wish to keep away from us. But not seeing what we are like we blame others. Unless we see that we are behaving like this we cannot change. Other people realise what we are like : as we are, we do not - until we begin to observe ourselves. Through not seeing what we are like, we believe we are not properly treated.

If we observe what we are thinking and feeling, what we are saying, how we are acting, after a time a new memory begins, a memory about ourselves. From then on, we begin to realise we are *not* what we supposed ourselves to be. We will begin to behave differently, not to blame other people, not to feel owed something. We will begin to realise we are two people and always have been. What we have supposed ourselves to be is imaginary.

1

When we see the contradictions between our imaginary 'ourselves', and what we really are, we begin to change, because we are being parted from the illusion of ourselves. We begin to realise that we have rested on an entirely false basis.

When we observe what we are really like we make ourselves open to receive help - help that can really change us. Help cannot reach us while we are self-satisfied.

This Work says that help exists for those who begin to realise, in every daily act, in everything said and felt, that they are not really what they suppose themselves to be.

When we begin to observe ourselves sincerely our whole fate begins to change. But this means noticing, over a long period, the way we talk, the way we think, the criticisms we make, the resentment of what is said to us, the way we react to others, the opinions from which we argue, the way we are flattered, how we judge others, our vanity, cruelty, moods, emotions. Unless we detach ourselves from these things, we remain mechanical.

Our psychic life, our inner life, is in darkness, until we begin to let in a ray of light, of consciousness of what is going on there. For this to happen we have to divide ourselves in two - an observing part, and an observed part. When Observing 'I' is established in us, it is from this 'I' that everything else follows. It is small and weak to begin with, but it is like a window to let in light.

TWO

The object of Self-Observation is to enable us to change ourselves. But its first object is to make us more conscious of ourselves. Only by making ourselves more conscious to ourselves does it enable us to begin to change.

In ordinary life we see only what is outside us, and do not notice what is going on inside us, how we think, and feel, and speak, always in the same way. But we have an internal sense. It is undeveloped, but it can be developed, and begin to show us what we are like - and thereby we can be changed.

We cannot be changed unless we see the kind of person we are. We practise Self-Observation in order to increase our consciousness, and without an increase in consciousness nothing in ourselves - or in mankind - can be changed.

The practical side of this Work begins with Self-Observation, and not with trying to change outer circumstances or other people : but it must be uncritical Self-Observation.

We have naturally a small degree of Self-Observation, but it never gets beyond a certain point. We begin to criticise ourselves. We stop and begin to put ourselves in the right, to restore the ordinary feeling of ourselves. We have to pass beyond this point, and have the strength to bear what we observe, calmly. This is difficult because we are identified, attached to ourselves and, naturally, are only concerned not to be foolish or ridiculous.

We have to observe, not only that we have done something wrong, but what happens inside us afterwards. There can be no change in us if we are stopped by self-criticism.

In order to begin to observe oneself begin with something specific; for instance, talking or behaving under certain circumstances. We must get to know these things thoroughly, objectively, without criticising. When we notice that words come out of our mouths willy-nilly we begin to see that we have no consciousness, and that there is something *not ourselves* in us, which we cannot check.

We have to study ourselves as if we were another person independent of ourselves.

Man is mechanical, the Work says, and he reacts to life mechanically. The first step in changing oneself is to realise gradually that what one takes as oneself is a machine.

We do not see into ourselves. We are living in a state of internal darkness, and nothing can be changed unless we let light into this darkness. We imagine we know ourselves. But we are reacting automatically to life at every moment.

Self-Observation shows us this bit by bit; and Self-Observation, by letting in light, begins the change in us by its own action: for this light is consciousness, provided that it is uncritical.

The illusion that we are conscious, and that we are one, prevent us from changing. We believe we have a permanent, unchanging 'I'. First we must observe ourselves uncritically.

When we begin to realise that things speak out of us and actions take place from us without our consciousness, we begin to get a new view of ourselves. But we think we know and that we remember, until Self-Observation shows us that we are not what we imagine but are machines. Then, uncritical Self-Observation will prevent many things from taking place in us, and show us what is not us at all. It is being asleep to ourselves that makes us go on behaving as we do.

This Work begins with oneself, and its aim is to change oneself. We miss the point if we think it is about external affairs. Everyone is a point of possible change, and change, whether of oneself or of the world lies here. If we change, we make room for others. But we cannot change unless we observe ourselves. We are deluded by thinking that what is outside us should be changed.

Through our attitude to others all kinds of frictions arise, and we do not see that we are responsible for the situation. But we can become aware that we criticise, and that what others said of us is true. This would mean that we had observed ourselves sufficiently to become more conscious of ourselves and it is this that alters a situation.

Self-Observation is to make us more conscious of ourselves, and this is the starting-point of this system called the Work.

THREE

Change means to change what one is now. One can no longer retain the same opinions or judge others in the same way. It is not to add to what one is, but to change one's being.

From this Work, man is regarded as not conscious. The first increase of consciousness we can develop is through real self-knowledge, by means of Self-Observation.

We imagine we are fully conscious. We live - the Work says - in a world of sleeping humanity, and we ourselves are asleep. Anything can happen in this world, and everything does merely *happen*. It always will, unless we wake up. If we could awaken, a new world would become possible.

First this requires the acknowledgment that we are asleep, and then the giving up of the illusions and pictures of oneself.

All our theories of improving the world, while we are still asleep, merely intensify the sleep of humanity.

There are

Four states of consciousness actual and possible to man :

Diagram

4   State of Objective Consciousness

3   State of Self-Awareness of Self-Consciousness or Self-Remembering (First truly waking state)

2   So-called Waking State

1   Sleep with dreams

In the first state of consciousness we are acutally asleep in bed. In the second state of consciousness we walk about the world, occupied with our daily affairs, thinking we are awake. But the third state of consciousness is the first truly waking state, and is actually our right. The fourth state is consciousness of the truth of things as they are.

Unless we can attain the third state of consciousness we cannot receive help. Help can only reach us when we realise we are asleep. Man asleep cannot obtain help.

THE WORK IDEA OF HELP

We can get help if we work on ourselves, and through Self-Remembering raise the level of consciousness in ourselves to a higher state. Then help can reach us. When on realises one is asleep one realises one must have help.

There is a Work parable that illustrates the situation of man at present. Mankind is fast asleep, and is walking towards the edge of a precipice that it does not see. But an individual man can wake up to the realisation that he is on the edge of a precipice; and if he were to open his eyes to this he would see that there is a rope above his head which he can climb up : but in order to reach this rope he has to jump. When we are on the level where we imagine we can be helped *as we are,* no help can reach us.

For anything better to exist we must change ourselves. Complacency, self-satisfaction, vanity, ignorance - all these and many other things prevent help from reaching us.

Prayer was originally to ask for help to lift one to a higher level of consciousness. The Lord's Prayer is designed to make a man remember himself, for an entire change of his being, so that help can enter him.

The nature of help is, first, to show us where we are wrong. This Work teaches that there is help, but it only touches a man and makes its presence known when he lifts himself up to it, that is,when he lifts himself up to the third state of consciousness. If we really feel our situation, we will try to lift ourselves to a new level of consciousness.

FOUR

Help exists but can only reach the third level of consciousness - called the state of Self-Consciousness, or Self-Awareness, or Self-Remembering. This is the first truly waking state.

To become conscious we have to begin to observe ourselves; we have to observe what we are saying, what we are thinking, what we are feeling, what sensations we are having, what our movements are.

We have to observe ourselves aright, from a definite starting-point, in a definite direction. First, that we are not one, but many. We are a thinking man; an emotional man; a moving man; an instinctive man who feels hungry, thirsty, hot or cold, well or ill.

All these are separately controlled by what the Work calls *centres*. Intellectual centre controls our thinking, and emotional centre controls what emotions we feel; moving centre controls all the movements of the body, and instinctive centre looks after all the inner workings of the body, such as the digestion of food, the circulation of the blood, breathing, and sensation.

We often think one thing and feel another because the different centres do not work in harmony. If a man observes himself only in relation to intellectual centre and emotional centre he will see that he is two people and not one.

The mind of moving centre works differently from the mind of intellectual centre - for instance, the moving activity of the hands when playing the piano, in contrast to the intellectual activity of the mind when thinking and conversing.

The working of the body is controlled by instinctive centre. It looks after all the inner work of the organisation of the body of which intellectual centre knows nothing.

If we wish to know ourselves in the right way to be more conscious of ourselves, we must first observe these four men in ourselves. Take for instance getting up early, and the difficulties involved, showing we are not a unity.

This shows how intellectual centre cannot by itself control other centres. Two centres must be in agreement to control a third.

The first stage in self-change then is to realise that *one is not one person.* We must realise we are four different people; four people with different minds.

Each centre has a certain amount of force available to it at a particular time to work it. If this force is used up it cannot do its work properly. We cannot go on using one centre for as long as we fancy. The force is exhausted. But we can then use another centre. Everything we do takes force - thinking, feeling, moving about, eating, drinking. Mechanically we act from the centre which is stored with force and is attracted by something. We must understand that if we are exhausted in one centre it is possible to use the force in another.

Our lives are distributed over the centres. Each has its different interests which are not antagonistic but complementary to each other, and each is necessary for human life. Balanced Man means a man in whom all centres work normally and have their right periods of activity.

Now the intellectual and moving centres can be made to act by direct effort. We can work out a problem, concentrate on something, or do some muscular task. But we *cannot make* ourselves have a particular emotion, or *make* ourselves hungry, cold, hot, etc. To a certain extent we can resist an emotion or sensation, but we cannot direct what kind of emotion or sensation we have.

FIVE

All men have Intellectual Centre, Emotional Centre, and the Instinctive and Moving Centres, but in different men these centres are very differently developed.

First example : take a man who likes activity and a man who likes to think - a Number 1 Man and a Number 3 Man. If they try to meet they each wish to talk of things which arise from their predominating centres. They are alike in that they both have the same centres, but they are unlike in that one has developed in Moving Centre and the other in Intellectual Centre.

Humanity is divided into three types of man - Number 1 Man, Number 2 Man, and Number 3 Man. Number 1 Man has to be further classified according to whether he is:

Number 1 Moving - whose primary concern is with action and muscular work.

Number 1 Instinctive - whose primary concern is for physical comfort, and who will be lazy and inactive.

The Majority of mankind is either Number 1 Instinctive or Number 1 Moving Man.

Number 2 is emotional man who *feels* everything. At one moment he is enthusiastic and exalted, the next he is depressed and moody. He is concerned with his likes and dislikes. His life swings between hope and despair, enthusiasm and dejection, love and hate, like and dislike.

Number 3 is intellectual man. His centre of gravity lies in Intellectual Cente, he is a theorist, with a theory about everything. His own thoughts and other people's recorded thoughts interest him more than anything else.

Each of these three men is characterised by having one centre mainly at work. An educated man, however, is not merely 1,2 or 3; the other centres to a certain extent work in him.

First example: take a Number 1 (moving) 2 3 Man - a soldier. His emotions make him moody or sensitive or jealous. He is pre-occupied with himself, and not good at exams.

Second example: take a Number 1 (instinctive) 3 2 Man. He is also a soldier, fond of sport. But he studies the history of wars, and strategy, and perhaps non-military subjects. He gets through exams quite easily; but he *feels* little, is not upset or moody, but a harsh disciplinarian.

So six formulations of man can be made: 1 2 3, 1 3 2; 2 1 3, 2 3 1; 3 1 2, 3 2 1. A 1 2 3 (instinctive) Man is concerned chiefly with eating, will be lazy and disinclined to make effort. Governed by his body, he will be easily depressed, become sulky and moody. Such a man hardly thinks at all.

Which of these men we are can only be found out by Self-Observation. *But proper approach to life necessitates the proper working of all centres* - and to approach situations with the wrong centre is useless.

Each centre requires its own development.

Mechanical Humanity is lopsided because life is viewed through one centre only; and consequently the people belonging to the mechanical circle of humanity do not understand one another.

The aim and object of this Work is to reach Balanced Man, Number 4 Man. Number 4 Man has all the centres more or less equally developed, so that one centre does not usurp the function of another, and each centre does its own work as may be appropriate to the situation.

To reach Number 4 Man it is necessary to *work on oneself consciously.* Number 4 Man is not mechanical. People who have begun to reach the level of Number 4 Man begin, at the same time, to understand one another.

To begin to approach Number 4 Man a person must be willing to develop those sides of himself which are lacking in development. Therefore no new experience is useless, once one understands the direction in which evolution lies.

In life people do not understand one another because they have no common language. The first step to understanding one another is to learn a common language.

SIX

We have seen that man is not one, but four, each centre in him being a different mind. He is in fact multiple. Over a long period Self-Observation will show us this multitude, to each of which we say 'I'.

At every moment these 'I's change: now one, now another speaks, and one may contradict another, or at least know nothing of what the first 'I' said.

We ascribe to ourselves many things which we do *not* possess such as full consciousness, will, and a real, permanent 'I' that never changes.

This is illusion. Man has not one will but many contradictory wills. Man is not conscious, but lives almost all his life asleep. He has not a permanent 'I' but a multitude of 'I's. Man is compared in a Work allegory to *'A House in Disorder'*. The Master is away, and the servants are doing what they like. When the telephone rings, they speak and pretend that they are the Master, and make all sorts of promises and orders under this pretence. Some of these servants feel that there is a better state possible. They see clearly what is going on, and band together with the intention of putting order in the house, in the hope that this will attract the return of the Master.

Each 'I' in a man has been acquired from some experience in life, from imitation, from environment, from something real, from fantasy, from profession, etc.

Man is not born with Personality, but with Essence. Personality begins to form itself very early in life, as soon as the child begins to imitate. At this point it acquires affectations, mannerisms, etc. Eventually the child takes as himself all that has been acquired.

Observing oneself from the standpoint of many 'I's, we begin to realise it is not the same person always speaking, though we call it 'I'. We notice that different 'I's speak at different times of the day, taking charge of us. We are changing all the time. Some 'I's are waking up, some 'I's are going to sleep. One 'I' makes a promise that other 'I's know nothing about. Some 'I's are very dangerous, and if we want to develop we have to prevent them from taking charge. These are especially the 'I's that twist things, that lie about everything, that are revengeful or bitter, that are full of self-pity or malice.

A baby is born as Essence, and is awake in so far as it really is Essence. It is of course small, but quite real. But, being born amongst sleeping people, it soon falls asleep. It begins to imitate, and that is one reason why Personality is formed.

Try to observe yourself from the standpoint of different 'I's existing in you, and notice how they often contradict one another. Notice the 'I's you are in when you are alone: notice how they change when anyone comes into the room. Try to notice the intonation with which different 'I's speak.

SEVEN

Unless we see what factor *in ourselves* stands in our way we cannot grow, cannot undergo an inner development. If we wish to develop we have to be able to observe ourselves.

It is usual to see all our difficulties as being due to causes outside ourselves, because this is all we do see. But if we begin to realise that it is ourselves, our level of being, that attracts our life, and understand the necessity of working on ourselves because our problem lies in ourselves, we can begin to change. If we can come to the point of realising that our problems lie in ourselves, we know that everything depends on our efforts to change ourselves. And unless we come to this point of consciousness everything will remain, not merely the same, but will get worse.

We must try to discover by Self-Observation what it is that keeps us in the same place in ourselves.

To change life means to change ourselves. But mostly, we have the illusion that change for the improvement of our life depends on outer circumstances, and that those ought to be different. This is what makes us unhappy.

The first thing we have to do to change ourselves is to give up our suffering. But people won't - they struggle to keep it.

The Work says that the world is governed not by sex or power, but by negative emotions - that is by certain states of the emotional centre, called negative emotions. This refers to suffering. Unless we give up suffering, we cannot change. The first sign of wrong attitude to life, the first illusion, is useless suffering. This happens because we approach life through our own ideas of what it ought to be, and imagine that what happens to us is exceptional. All this produces suffering, because we have not understood the nature of life, and don't wish to know. We struggle with difficulties - yes - but think of our lives as spoiled.

We therefore come to a new standpoint: that of realising our lives are spoiled by suffering, and wishing to be rid of all useless self-pity, and the sense of grievance and despondency. We have to feel that life owes us nothing, and other people owe us nothing. On the contrary we have to feel that we owe to others and owe to life more than we can repay. In the words of the Lord's Prayer, properly translated, we should ask for our debts to be cancelled, 'as we cancel the debts owed to us', not 'forgive'. As we eliminate from ourselves the idea that we are owed something by others, so do we become free. The feeling of being owed is useless suffering. When we struggle with this we are suffering *usefully*.

This effort needs Work ideas. Life ideas encourage useless suffering, and in the end deprive us of pleasure, happiness and new interests.

To change oneself one must be free from petty attachments and forms of imagination about oneself that hold us in the position we are in in life. We are attached to everything in ourselves: vanity, stupidity, merit, beauty, elegance, accomplishments, self-evaluation, etc., and particularly to suffering. These must be weakened for a change to take place. Or it may be that we are attached to the other side of the same coin - to the idea of not being ambitious, of not bothering about life.

The Centres
Intellectual Centre is born with a negative part and a postiive part, as in order to think there must be a comparison - an ability to say 'yes' and 'no'.

The Emotional Centre is not born with a negative part - it should not be there, but it is acquired by the influence of people who are negative. By contact with adults a child learns to pity itself, to feel grievances, to speak crossly, to dwell on its misfortunes, to be melancholy, moody, irritable, suspicious, jealous, to hurt others, etc. This dreadful *infection* of a child is something against which nothing can be done because it is not clearly recognized. This infection forms the negative part in Emotional Centre. And this infection is handed on from generation to generation.

Negative emotions may take very subtle forms but eventually they all lead down to violence. Once negative emotion passes beyond a certain point it rouses deep-seated factors in the Instinctive Centre, and people then want to hurt and murder one another.

There is a particular reason why negative emotions are even worse than this. We have two Higher Centres in us - Higher Intellectual, and Higher Emotional - that are fully developed and working, but we are not in contact with them. When we feel a lack in ourselves, an emptiness, a sense of futility and of being lost in a world we do not understand, it is due to the fact that we cannot hear Higher Centres. But if we made contact with Higher Centres in our ordinary state, our lower centres would be rendered a thousand times worse, more intense.

We can live in a better world, in this world, if negative emotions are reduced to a minimum.

If, after having observed our negative emotions, we struggle with our emotional life, we shall see that our whole attitude to life needs changing. It is impossible to overcome negative emotions alone, because they are involved in our whole attitude to life! Every situation needs a new standpoint by which to think of it; our whole idea of ourselves has to be changed, and this is *work on oneself*. The Work is designed to put us in touch with Higher Centres, but while we are governed by negative emotions, the influences coming from Higher Centres cannot reach us.

EIGHT

From the standpoint of this Teaching, man is not one - he is not a unity. From the point of view of centres he is three : an intellectual man, an emotional man, and an instinctive-moving man.

The Work also speaks of man in terms of knowledge and being. These two sides form him - he is both, not merely his knowledge, nor merely his being.

First, consider *Being*. Different kinds of animals have different being. The being of a snake is different from that of a grasshopper, and the being of a grasshopper from that of a pig; and a pig has different being from the being of a tiger. A carpenter selects his wood according to its suitability for a job. If some stock of wood has not matured rightly he will say something to the effect that its 'nature' has gone out of it. He is talking about being.

It is not difficult to realise that people have different kinds of knowledge, but it is not easy to realise that they have different kinds of being. The conception of being is emphasized in the Work, and we must try to realise what being is, and why the concept is so stressed.

First example : A man of superior *knowledge* in his field, but who does all kinds of mean and petty acts, is full of envy, cheats, steals information without acknowledging it. Although this is obvious to us he does not realise it and is astonished that people do not like him. Without understanding that this man has two sides - knowledge and being - we shall be baffled by him. We dislike his being, and we can describe his *level of being as* such and such.

Second example : A man has no particular knowledge, but is not malicious, is not mean and petty, does not cheat, keeps his word. Although in knowledge he is undeveloped, his *level of being* is higher than the first man's.

If we value only knowledge, we shall admire the first man, whatever he does, because of his knowledge; and despise the second because he is ignorant.

This judgement will define us, because we shall then have poor being.

This is the tendency today, to make heroes of criminals. But a criminal cannot be taught because his level of being will always use his knowledge in a criminal way.

We make use of our knowledge according to our level of being. For instance - two people with harmful knowledge of a third person : it is their level of being which determines their behaviour.

From this we can see that knowledge and being are different, and that our relation to our knowledge is governed by our being. To give knowledge to a person of being lower than his knowledge, results in its misuse.

The Work teaches that our knowledge and being should have equal development. If the two are approximately equal, the result is that we understand our knowledge.

Understanding is defined as the resultant of knowledge and being. Knowledge by itself, being by itself - neither alone gives understanding. We can know a lot and understand nothing. We can develop on the side of being to a point, and yet be stupid or ignorant.

In order to change, we must develop on the side of knowledge and on the side of being. If we only study the system intellectually, nothing will change. If we try to work on being without studying the knowledge, we will come to a stop. There will be no increase of understanding. When we begin to understand what we did not understand before, there is the chance of change precisely through the understanding.

A man is his understanding, and he cannot develop save through his understanding.

It is said that *our level of being attracts our life,* and that if we wish our life to be different a change in our level of being is necessary. That means that as long as our being stays the same the same kind of things will happen to us, no matter the place or the circumstances.

We can see that knowledge and being are relative in different people. Relativity of knowledge can be understood, but relativity of being is more difficult to understand.

NINE

Man is regarded as unfinished, incomplete, imperfect. He has the possibility of completing himself, perfecting himself, and all that is necessary for this lies in him.

He is an experiment in self-evolution. As he is mechanically, he is incomplete and undeveloped, but is capable of a further inner development. For this reason it is said that man is a *self-developing organism.*

In the New Testament man is compared to a seed. It is said that unless a man dies to what he is now, he cannot evolve into what is possible for him. A definite *transformation* is being spoken about by which the experiment can be completed. The idea that man is a self-developing organism means that he cannot develop under compulsion. To see God in the flesh would mean man being compelled to believe by the evidence of the senses, but man cannot develop in this way at all. He can only develop through understanding.

If man is a *special experiment* on this earth, as distinct from the animals which cannot undergo an individual evolution, what does it mean? It means that a man can only develop internally if he begins to understand the necessity of it, and seeks for the means himself. It is only through internal freedom, which is one's understanding, that a man can evolve. No external compulsion can bring this about. When we see we are wrong and realise what we are like and how we behave, then from this basis self-evolution becomes possible. We begin to change when we begin to understand ourselves, and see the need.

Man is free to change himself through his own understanding. This is the only sense in which he is free - and this freedom no-one can take from him. No-one can change life, or other people; but each person can change himself. This system begins with a man, with oneself, with you - and its object is to change *you yourself.*

No rules, rituals, ceremonies or regulations, even if their aim is to develop man, can change him unless he begins to understand.

The Work therefore begins by teaching that we must try to enter into ourselves, and begin to see ourselves. Prayers, pilgrimages etc., are useless because they are taken externally. It is only through new knowledge and work on our being that new understanding can be born.

The next idea is that *man is in a bad situation* on this earth. The earth is a small point in the solar-system, the solar-system a small point in the Milky Way or Galaxy, and the Galaxy is only one of many Galaxies. Man is in a bad position under many laws which do not necessarily contribute to his well-being. Cosmically speaking, man is a small thing in the universe, a new experiment which might be wiped out in favour of another experiment. Man becomes of consequence only when he realises his meaning and destiny and begins to live more consciously.

If man were only a machine he would not suffer his inner painful doubts and uncertainties, simply because he would then *be* a machine: but everyone knows in a dim way that this is not the case - and that they should be different.

The third idea about man is that as long as he remains asleep and mechanical *he is used.*

If man were incapable of doing anything about himself, his position would be without hope - he would be subject to all that happens around him, floods, disease, war etc. It would be his sole life. But if man is created a self-developing organism life cannot fulfil him and is not supposed to fulfil him : his full meaning is not in life. But life uses us owing to our position on this planet. Re-arrangement of outer things still leaves us under the same laws that use man. As long as being remains the same, mankind attracts the same kind of life, recurrently. The only starting-point of change is in us - in our spirit.

All mankind is asleep from the point of view of this system. We are asleep, and in this state mankind can do nothing. Today mankind is being used more and more by cosmic forces outside him because he has discarded the power to awaken.

This system turns round the central point that man is a self-developing organism, capable of evolving through his understanding, and changing his level of being - by which means he can come under new influences and reach help.

In the first two states of consciousness we are mechanical and cannot change. Only at the Third Level of Consciousness, or Self-Remembering, can man alter his situation on this earth.

TEN

('The more our outward man dies away, the more living is the inward' : St Paul).

Man consists of two parts, Essence and Personality. Essence is the part that can grow.

At birth a person is Essence, but it is undeveloped. The baby has to grow, and each centre has to develop its mind and intelligence. A baby lives in Instinctive Centre: little by little it begins to develop in Moving Centre - to walk. It understands scarcely anything. Life is at a great distance from it, and it lives in its own world. When it begins to speak and understand something of what people are saying, life comes nearer. Personality begins to be formed.

Life comes in as impressions, which fall on the different centres, and form *rolls*. Impressions are deposited on rolls in the different centres. At birth the centres are blank, save the Instinctive Centre, and a small part of Moving Centre.

Everything we have learnt is stored in these Centres. All our habits - mental, emotional and physical - are stored in these rolls. By means of these rolls Personality is built.

People with similar rolls may feel connected, and those with dissimilar ones may feel at a loss with one another. But people who have different rolls, who differ in Personality, may feel drawn to one another : in such cases it is some similarity in Essence.

We have to understand that Essence is very soon surrounded by Personality. What we are born with is surrounded by what we acquire - beliefs, opinions, customs, etc. What we are taught forms Personality. What Essence is, what we really are, remains undeveloped. But a man only grows through a new growth of Essence.

If in life we wish to be the foremost authority on some subject, and study to do so, we increase Personality. If we do something solely to be first, all our efforts lead solely to a growth of Personality - and this will be at the expense of Essence.

In Esoteric teaching, man is regarded as a seed capable of individual development. The part of man that can grow, as a seed, is Essence. But during our upbringing, our sense of ourselves, our feeling of 'I', gradually shifts from what we really are to what we acquire from life. Strictly speaking Essence is what *we are*. Personality is what is *not us*.

Through a vague feeling of this, people sometimes try to avoid life. But though it is true that simple people are more essential, their Essence has not developed beyond a certain point. Their understanding remains that of a child.

The Work says that Essence is capable of only a very small development by itself. In order to grow beyond a certain point, it must have food. An acorn feeds first on the substance that surrounds the germ of life contained in it. When it has developed as a plant, it draws nourishment from the sun and the earth. With us, the point is to form food in us that later can feed Essence. This food is the Personaltiy. Unless Personality forms itself round Essence by the action of life, Essence cannot grow further than a certain point.

Essence can grow by itself up to four, five or six, say. It then stops. A child then leaves its Essence and becomes more and more immersed in the slowly forming Personality. It is taught what to believe in, what is useful, and so on - a confusion of things.

But this Work says, despite this, that Personality must be formed; because if we wish at a later stage of life to grow individually, we cannot do so without this food of Personality. We can only grow at the expense of Personality.

What is the inner situation of man, as regards his possible individual development? Man is created a self-developing organism. The real development is the development of what is really him, what he was born with, the growth of Essence.

Through education and external circumstances in general, and through imagination, Personality takes charge of us. Personality becomes active and Essence passive. This means that we believe in all we have imitated - this side we have acquired, and take as ourselves. It can be to the extent that all that is real in us practically dies.

Nevertheless, Personality must form itself in a man to relate him to life, and the richer the Personality, the better. But it is only a step *towards* development. Development *begins* when all this food is made disposable to Essence for its further growth. In other words, the development of Essence can only take place at the expense of Personality, and of certain results of its formation in us. We can only grow by making Personality passive. This enables the Essence little by little to become active and grow.

So if we desire to change, we have to begin to go against ourselves in a certain way - against what we take to be ourselves. All the psychological teaching of this system is connected with the central idea of *a development of Essence at the expense of Personality* - a development that is impossible unless Personality has been formed first of all, since it depends on Personality for its fulfilment, and particularly on the quality of the food that is stored in Personality.

ELEVEN

The question of the development of Essence does not lie in trying to find what in Essence itself should develop.

It is not a matter of making Essence develop as it were by force, but of allowing it to develop. Essence cannot develop because it is surrounded by Personality.

A particular side of Personaltiy is False Personality. It is said that False Personality is constructed out of imagination. Imagination is one of the most powerful forces acting on our inner life, in the inner world of reality in which we live. Take an example of, in early years, reading a book and imagining oneself the hero - we believe ourselves to be what imagination tells us. When imagination has been consented to, a false feeling of oneself is created, a false feeling of 'I'. This is the basis of False Personality.

As we grow up and Personality is formed, instead of being ourselves, we cease to be ourselves and gradually become an invented person. The centre-of-gravity of the feeling of ourselves passes into the artificial feeling of 'I' which is composed of imagination.

For the essential feeling of oneself is substituted a misleading feeling of 'I'. It is this invented side, this Imaginary 'I' or False Personality that prevents Essence from growing later on in life.

False Personality is our self-liking, self-love, self-admiration, and the source of self-pity and negative emotions.

The development of Essence after Personality has been formed depends on rendering False Personality and Imaginary 'I' passive. That means that we have to discover by Self-Observation what is real and what is false in us. For in Personaltiy there is both much that is useful and much that is useless. But we have to see that we imagined ourselves first in some grand walk of life, and are actually ordinary.

As False Personality is composed of imagination we must try to observe some of its forms. Try to observe lying - for instance telling a story in such a way as to put oneself in a favourable position, to make oneself appear more clever or more in the right than one is. We don't like admitting we are wrong.

We are the slave of our Imaginary 'I', for at all costs we feel bound to keep it alive and defend it both from others and ourselves. Consequently we are always lying - by boasting, justifying and pretending. And we seek the satisfaction of being taken seriously by other people, by asking for praise and encouragement. If we fail in this, we feel depressed and hurt, or hate people.

The False Personality in people injures relationships: they cannot be real, for it is pretence of the imagination. If the Essence of one person is attracted by another's Essence something real is possible - if Personality does not ruin the situation.

A child, from being real in its early years, is then, from the necessity of having to meet outer life, forced to imitate other people. It begins to be something not itself, and to believe in it. The feeling of 'I' passes outwards into the growing Personality, and owing to this formation of Personality there is nothing real in the sense of this feeling of 'I'. Everything the child imitates and invents concerning itself forms many different 'I's. So when grown-up we are a conglomeration of 'I's which may act in different ways at different times.

But Imaginery 'I' or False Personality acts in such a way as to make us believe that we are one and the same person at all times. We are sure that we have a single, unchanging and permanent 'I'. Unless we realise we are not like this we cannot change. For we also believe that we have Real Will and can 'do'.

But we are a 'house in disorder'. We are many people each with a desire - not one person with one will. This is why we cannot 'do'. Only a man with real individuality has a Real Will and can do.

When we begin to observe ourselves with the aim of seeing different personalities, the power of Imaginary 'I' begins to be weakened. We see we are different from what

27

we imagined ourselves to be. When we really *see* the different 'I's speaking, an illusion about ourselves begins to tbe destroyed, and we pass a little nearer to the state in which Real 'I' can come nearer.

As long as False Personality is in power Essence will be incapable of growth. But once we begin to realise our situation Essence is no longer held in check. Our inner situation begins to alter, and as Personality becomes passive, so does Essence develop and become active.

TWELVE

PERSONAL EFFORTS A MAN MUST MAKE

In order to change himself, a man must work on himself. But there are both useful and useless efforts. As an example of useless effort, take the instance of an irritable man who, hearing of this system and not understanding it, gives up smoking. The result is that he becomes even more irritable.

Effort must be intelligent, and it must be based on the direction the Work teaches, and on what we have observed in ourselves in relation to the Teaching.

Unless we have observed ourselves and seen what we have to work on, nothing useful can result from any efforts we may make. If one has observed one is irritable, one is in a position to work on oneself usefully.

All efforts made must be useful in three respects - to the Work itself, or to others in the Work, or to oneself.

The First Line of Work is to change the kind of person one is. The Second Line of Work is in connection with one's neighbours - those with whom one is working, who are nearest in understanding. The Third Line of Work concerns the Work itself. For instance, we must think of what might harm it and what might help it, and realise that if we behave badly or talk badly we harm the Work itself and other people in it - and ourselves, so that without seeing the reason we can no longer work on ourselves.

The Teaching lays down these three lines of Work. No-one can work only for himself.

The first useful effort we can make is the effort of Self-Observation - learning to observe ourselves *uncritically*. This requires great and continual effort, because it must be done consciously. Try to observe for a short, given period, for we have not the force to observe longer, thoughts, emotions, sensations, movements. It is necessary to find the right state internally, where we really want to observe and realise that we can, by seeing, for instance, that we think one thing and feel something quite different.

Ordinarily we are identified with everything that takes place within us - every thought, mood, sensation, emotion. This means that we take it as ourselves. We put the feeling of 'I' into it, and for this reason nothing can change in us.

Let us return to the irritable man. Suppose he fully observes his irritation - then his situation has changed, because instead of being identified and being his irritation, he is to a certain extent separated from it. He is separated because he can observe it as something which is not himself. He can see it as an object. He has drawn out of it some of the feeling of 'I', and the greater the power of his Self-Observation, the less power will the irritation have over him. He is no longer so identified with himself.

This has been brought about by the establishment of Observing-I - the first step in making a new system in us, which is the first practical aim of the Teaching.

The greatest hindrance to self-evolution is that we are constantly identified with what attracts our attention at a given moment. And for this reason we forget ourselves. But our natural right is the third state of consciousness, the state of Self-Remembering. Unless we can begin to Self-Remember, we are identified with everything. We thus live in a state of inner disorder, identifying with our surroundings. That is why we are said to be asleep. We are so accustomed to identification that we only feel the taste of being identified.

When we identify with a problem, a person, a feeling, a situation, we put ourselves under its power. We are mastered by it. Self-mastery begins with struggling with identifying.

It is possible, too, to identify with working on oneself, by forgetting that one's small aim is not everything. Aim must not be done publicly; that causes identifying and gives no result.

It is particularly difficult to free ourselves from identifying because we feel our best work is done by being identified.

By being identified we see only one side of a question. If we are instinctive man, for instance, we identify with the food we are especially fond of. Instinctive Man becomes the steak he eats. We become whatever we identify with - money, woes, hatred, etc., and cannot remember ourselves.

To remember ourselves we must not identify. To learn how not to identify we must first not be identified with ourselves. For this reason we must learn and practise Self-Observation. When we realise we need not go with a mood etc., but can draw the feeling of 'I' out of it, we begin to see what not identifying with ourselves means.

BIBLIOGRAPHY

Informal Work Talks and Teachings 1940-1950 by Maurice Nicoll. October 1995. ISBN 0 948333 51 0.   £ 8.95

Simple Explanation of Work Ideas by Maurice Nicoll. February 1994. ISBN 0 948333 31 6. 2nd edition Sept 1995. ISBN 1 85398 081 1.
                                                                    £ 5.95

Practical Work Tasks by Beryl Pogson. May 1995.
ISBN 0 948333 47 2   £ 5.95

Centenary Fragments by Beryl Pogson. December 1994.
ISBN 0 948333 36 7.   £15.95

Unforgotten Fragments by Beryl Pogson. March 1994.
ISBN 0 948333 29 4.   £15.95

Commentary on the Fourth Gospel by Beryl Pogson. Republished August 1993. ISBN 0 948333 19 7.   £ 5.95

The Work Life (Talks at Dorton House and Nutley Terrace) by Beryl Pogson. Republished by Samuel Weiser, Box 612, York Beach, Maine 0310. USA. August 1994. ISBN 0 87728-809-7.   £ 9.99

Work Talks at Brighton 1963 to 1966 by Beryl Pogson. Republished November 1993. ISBN 0 948333 23 5.   £ 5.95

Work Talks at The Dicker 1966 by Beryl Pogson. Republished December 1993. ISBN 0 948333 24 3.   £ 8.95

More Work Talks 1966 by Beryl Pogson. Republished January 1994. ISBN 0 948333 26 X.   £ 5.95

Maurice Nicoll: A Portrait by Beryl Pogson. (Published by Vincent Stuart 1961, re-published 1987 by Fourth Way Books, New York)£ 9.95

In the East my Pleasure Lies An Esoteric Interpretation of Some Plays of Shakespeare; *Three Plays by Shakespeare; The Royalty of Nature:* A commentary of Shakespeare's History Plays by Beryl Pogson. Republished January 1994. ISBN 0 948333 27 8.   £15.95

Work Teaching - Work Poems. Ronald & Muriel Oldham. Republished September 1993. ISBN 0 948333 22 7.   £ 5.95

Sale of Books to benefit : MACMILLAN NURSES
Cancer Relief Macmillan Fund Anchor House 15 Britten Street London SW3 3TZ

"The best ideas are usually so simple it seems hard to believe they didn't always exist."

PERSONAL INDEX AND NOTES

PERSONAL INDEX AND NOTES

PERSONAL INDEX AND NOTES

PERSONAL INDEX AND NOTES

PERSONAL INDEX AND NOTES

PERSONAL INDEX AND NOTES